EMPOWERED LIVING

FAITH-BASED FOUNDATIONS FOR RECOVERY AND GROWTH

Robert McClellan

EMPOWERED LIVING
FAITH-BASED FOUNDATIONS FOR RECOVERY AND GROWTH

Robert McClellan

2025 All rights reserved. This publication may not be reproduced, stored in an electronic system, or transmitted in any form or by any means, electronic, mechanical, photocopy, recording, or otherwise, without proper credit to the author. Brief quotations may be used without permission.

Scriptures unless otherwise marked are taken from the KING JAMES VERSION (KJV): KING JAMES VERSION, public domain.

Scripture quotations are from the ESV® Bible (The Holy Bible, English Standard Version®), © 2001 by Crossway, a publishing ministry of Good News Publishers. Used by permission. All rights reserved. The ESV text may not be quoted in any publication made available to the public by a Creative Commons license.
The ESV may not be translated in whole or in part into any other language.

Scripture quotations taken from the Amplified® Bible (AMP), Copyright © 2015 by The Lockman Foundation. Used by permission. lockman.org

Scripture quotations marked (NLT) are taken from the Holy Bible, New Living Translation, copyright ©1996, 2004, 2015 by Tyndale House Foundation. Used by permission of Tyndale House Publishers, Carol Stream, Illinois 60188. All rights reserved.

ISBN: 978-1-961482-22-7

Empowered Living was created from lived experience with substance use disorder and the associated trauma. The lessons contained herein will serve as a guide to integrate faith with your recovery in a way that makes spirituality obtainable and easily understood. With over 20 years of sobriety under his belt, the author has developed methods and honed concepts that can specifically speak to someone in recovery. Come to the table with a willingness to learn, and you too can begin living an empowered life.

Foreword

It has been said that every journey begins with a single step, and for many who battle addiction, that step can feel heavier than any they have ever taken. It takes courage to admit a need, humility to ask for help, and faith to believe that life can be different. The pages that follow are not written by someone looking in from the outside, but by a voice that has walked the long road of recovery—facing its setbacks, celebrating its victories, and learning how faith makes freedom possible.

Empowered Living is more than a collection of lessons. It is a roadmap drawn from lived experience, time-tested truths, and a faith that has proven strong enough to carry the weight of struggle. With over two decades of sobriety, the author writes not with theory but with testimony. He understands the feelings of emptiness, the cycles of relapse, and the wounds that often drive people to numb their pain. But he also understands what happens when God's grace meets human weakness: chains are broken, identities are restored, and new life begins.

Here you will not be asked to chase an abstract "higher power." Instead, you are invited to meet the very Source of power—Jesus Christ. These lessons weave biblical truth into practical recovery principles clearly, compassionately, and accessibly. Each page is designed to help you build a solid foundation, embrace forgiveness, walk in a relationship with God, and discover the true freedom of living Spirit-empowered.

If you are willing to come with an open heart and a teachable spirit, you will discover that you are not alone. The same God who spoke the world into existence can speak peace into your storm. The same Savior who lifted others from brokenness is ready to lift you as well. Take these lessons seriously. Apply them. Pray through them. Let them reshape how you see yourself and how you see God.

My prayer is that Empowered Living will not simply be a book you read, but a journey you live. May these pages remind you that with Jesus Christ, recovery is not just survival—it is restoration, transformation, and a life truly empowered.

Larry Arrowood

INTRO

Welcome! We are so proud of you for making recovery a part of the next chapter of your life. Please take the time to get to know everyone around you. We are here to help.

Trusting people is never easy. However, you have found yourself among friends who share similar experiences in life and have made an effort to trust again, to love and be loved again.

We are ready with open arms, open ears, and open hearts to better understand your journey up to this point.

You don't have to do this alone anymore!

LESSON 1

A GOOD FOUNDATION

"FOR OTHER FOUNDATION CAN NO MAN LAY THAN THAT IS LAID, WHICH IS JESUS CHRIST."

1 CORINTHIANS 3:11 KJV

One would assume that if you are pursuing help that you are ready for a change. Change can be scary at times, and new things can even feel a bit overwhelming at first. So, take a deep breath and relax. Your group leaders are here for you, and remember, we've been right where you are before.

Let's start by making some commitments to each other. As your new friends, we will not judge you. We will not try to control or manipulate you. We want you to be in charge of your recovery, and we are only here to guide, support, and love you through this process. In turn, we ask that you keep an open mind and an open heart, and allow us to help you.

In other words, let's be open and honest with each other about your journey. It's all right to cry, it's all right to vent, it's all right to ask questions. And if at any time you need prayer, we'd be happy to pray with you.

Alright, now that we've made some commitments to one another, let's discuss the first step in building a better life: the foundation.

A building's most crucial element is its foundation. It's so important that a contractor will not even consider building on a site until the foundation has been inspected and completed. If not taken seriously, the contractor could build a beautiful structure only to watch it collapse. Likewise, the life you are meant to live must be built on a solid foundation.

At the start of this lesson, the Bible passage highlighted the best foundation one could ever build their life on: Jesus Christ.

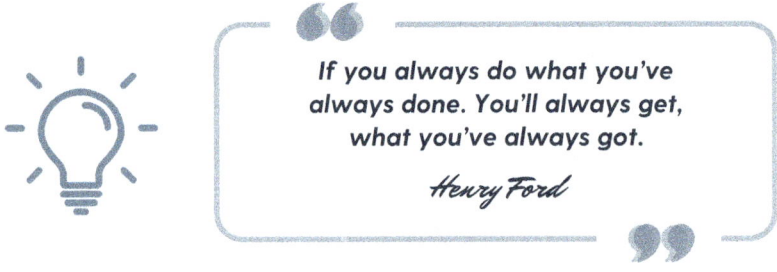

If you always do what you've always done. You'll always get, what you've always got.

Henry Ford

"**Jesus is the answer**" may seem like a simple phrase, but it is profoundly true. As you begin to build your life on Him, you will see just how powerful that statement really is.

There's a story in the Bible that you may relate to during this time in your life. It's found in the book of Luke, which says: "And when he had finished speaking, he said to Simon, "Put out into the deep and let down your nets for a catch." And Simon answered, "Master, we toiled all night and took nothing! But at your word, I will let down the nets." And when they had done this, they enclosed a large number of fish, and their nets were breaking." (Luke 5:4-6 ESV)

I'm sure you can relate to Simon in this story. He had tried to do things his way, and every effort only left him with empty nets. However, when he listened to and obeyed the word of the Master, his net was so full it nearly broke. If you've tried recovery your way, why not open God's word and let Him speak to you?

Statistics prove that faith-based programs work. However, many of these programs don't have a clear source for that faith. While some leave this topic open to interpretation, this program goes directly to the source of faith itself. We don't ask that you put your belief in a higher power; we ask that you put your trust in Jesus Christ, the Almighty and source of power itself.

Jesus is the foundation on which we will build an empowered life. He alone has power over any forces we are powerless to overcome. In this foundational level of recovery, there has to be a solid starting point—Jesus is that cornerstone you need.

(Read Ephesians 2:19-22 and 1 Peter 2:4-10)

$316 B
Faith-based volunteer support groups contribute up to $316.6 billion in savings to the US economy every year at no cost to tax payers.

84%
More than 84% of scientific studies show that faith is a positive factor in addiction prevention or recovery.

20K
An estimated 20,000+ lives are saved every year because of faith-based recovery programs in churches.

(1) Grim, B.J. & Grim, M.E. J Relig Health (2019) https://rdcu.be/bQIQE

PRACTICAL APPLICATIONS:

How can we replace the former foundations we've built our life on?
(Examples: Change of friends - 1st Corinthians 15:33, Replacing habits - Ephesians 2:1-10, Integrating Faith - Matthew 19:26)

_____
_____
_____
_____

What are some of the building blocks we could use to rebuild our life?
(Examples: Prayer, Bible study, Church community)

_____
_____
_____
_____

Who could you entrust as an accountability partner?

_____
_____
_____
_____

LESSON 2

RELATIONSHIP vs RELIGION

"BUT THE HOUR IS COMING, AND IS NOW HERE, WHEN THE TRUE WORSHIPERS WILL WORSHIP THE FATHER IN SPIRIT AND TRUTH…"

JOHN 4:23 ESV

We all have *"religion"* to an extent. We all give our devotion to something, or someone, and most of us feel that we are here for a reason. According to the Bible, *true religion* is not just a set of beliefs, rather it's a lifestyle. This often misunderstood word (*religion*) in our English vocabulary has an innate sense of good behind its definition. However, many bad things have been done in its name.

Throughout history, *"religion"* has started numerous wars, and it was under the banner of so called *"religion"* that the leaders of Jesus' day crucified their Messiah. When men became blinded by their religious zeal, they could not see that the very God that created the heavens and Earth stood in their midst.

So, what made the difference between the followers, and the foes, concerning Jesus of Nazareth?

One group looked at this man through the eyes of strict tradition and laws, they saw only a rule breaker, and refused to take the time to get to know Him personally. Others however, looked beyond what was seen on the surface and in doing so they saw to the heart of God. Some *knew of him*, while others took the time to *know him*.

> The LORD detests differing weights, and dishonest scales do not please him.
> *Proverbs 20:23 NIV*

One group had the truth, but could not perceive the spiritual. There must be a balance of spirit and truth, for (as our scripture introduction states) this is who is set apart as true worshippers. In other words, we need **relationship** coupled with our **religion**. Not one or the other, rather **both together**.

Jesus did not come to start a religion, He came to repair a relationship that was severed in the garden. When Adam was created, the Bible says that God breathed the breath of life into him, and **then** he became a living soul. Within all mankind is that connection with our Creator, it's His breath that fills our lungs when we are born.

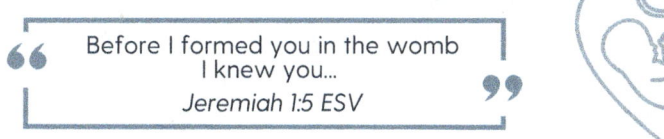

> " Before I formed you in the womb I knew you...
> *Jeremiah 1:5 ESV* "

After Adam fell prey to sin, that same living, breathing soul was separated from its Creator. Sin, by definition, is disobedience that results in separation from God. The curse of sin that Adam would endure was passed down to all of his blood relatives.

Therefore, the mission of Jesus was to remove the sin that separated us by conquering sin on the cross, and through His perfect blood, He would reverse the curse of sin for all mankind. Here's the good news! The sacrifice He made willingly was for everyone, not just for the Jewish people. This was always a part of His plan!

Knowing that we are created in His image and that the soul we have is *God-breathed* makes total sense of why we can hear a song about our Savior and tears will well up inside us. It's not just emotion; it is literally our soul crying out to be reunited with its Creator.

The woman He met at the well in our scripture setting (John 4) was a Samaritan. The Jews despised them because they were not of pure Jewish descent but were a mix of Gentile and Jew. The disciples of Jesus even questioned why He would want to travel through the city of Samaria for that reason. Religion said, "Jesus, don't talk to her; she is not one of God's chosen." Yet, the response of Jesus set them on their heels. Not only did He sit at the well where she was, but He also began speaking with her and even teaching her.

Here is where studying the Bible as a whole yields even more beauty to this historical account. Well over 400 years prior to this meeting, God promised Abraham this plot of land and later fulfilled that promise by leading Jacob to this very parcel of land. While living out this promise, it was dug by Jacob, hence its name (Jacob's Well), in the "parcel of ground" which he purchased from the sons of Hamor (Genesis 33:19).

Why is this so fascinating for us? Fast forward to this meeting with the woman at that same well, and we can see that God had actually been planning a meeting with this adulterous Samaritan woman for over 400 years!

If God was willing to traverse the span of several centuries, bypass the barriers created by religious culture, and travel hundreds of miles on foot to meet this one woman who, by all manmade standards, was deemed unworthy of God's love, how important we all must be in the eyes of our Creator!

That is the power of love and is the epitome of the perfect balance of *religion* and *relationship*. We see the response of this same love that met her where she was, yet loved her enough to not leave her as she was.

When we fully grasp this concept, we can begin to live a more confident life in Christ. It will also protect us from negative mindsets about our new life. By aiming for a balance of both Spirit and Truth we can eliminate harmful inner dialogue.

Religion	Relationship
I have to pray and read my Bible to make God happy.	I choose to pray and read my Bible to know God more.
I have to stop doing things that make God unhappy.	I choose to stop doing things that might separate me from God.
I will never be able to live up to what they want.	With His help I can be what He wants me to be.
If I mess up, everyone will be so disappointed.	He knows I'm trying and His opinion matters most.
I can never change.	I can do all things through Christ who gives me strength.

If you focus solely on religion, you may be disappointed in your experience with God. However, if you concentrate on building a relationship alongside your faith, everything will make more sense, and you can experience God at the level He intended for you. Biblically speaking, His intention has always been that mankind lives an empowered life.

PRACTICAL APPLICATIONS:

How can we worship Jesus in Spirit, and in Truth?
(Or how can we balance relationship and religion)

_____
_____
_____
_____
_____
_____

*Who is responsible for my relationship with God?
How does knowing this change my actions?*

_____
_____
_____
_____
_____
_____

*What did the story of the woman at the
well reveal about God to you?*

_____
_____
_____
_____
_____

LESSON 3

THE POWER OF FORGIVENESS

"FOR IF YE FORGIVE MEN THEIR TRESPASSES, YOUR HEAVENLY FATHER WILL ALSO FORGIVE YOU..."

MATTHEW 6:14 KJV

Words are a very powerful method of communication. With our words, we can choose to build someone up or tear someone down. We can describe things we see to another individual without them being able to physically see them for themselves. Almighty God used the spoken Word to bring everything we see into existence. God said, "Let there be," and there was. He shared that creative attribute with us by giving us the ability to communicate. This is most commonly felt in the songs we write, or in a beautiful poem that touches hearts. Yet, even normal everyday speech has an effect on the lives we live and the lives of those within our sphere of influence.

There are some powerful phrases in our language. Phrases like "I love you" and "I'm sorry" can literally end arguments and bind people together for life. In fact, throughout history, both war and peace have been achieved through mere words. That said, whether in letters written or words spoken, the power of words cannot be understated.

Perhaps one of the most powerful phrases that is rarely used is "I forgive you." Forgiveness requires mercy; it is opposed to our fallen human nature. Oftentimes, we are inhibited by pride, not understanding how free we can be.

> The pen is mightier than the sword.
> Edward Bulwer-Lytton

Sometimes, fear prevents us from expressing ourselves, as the person on the receiving end of those phrases may not acknowledge the weight of what those words mean to us when we say them. Worse still, they may not reciprocate the same feelings. Therefore, because it hurts to be wronged and because justice demands that the other party pays for their wrongdoing, the word "forgiveness" is not the first that comes to mind.

If you've lived a life of addiction, you know better than anyone what it means to be deeply hurt by someone and never hear the words "I'm sorry." One simple sentence can feel like medicine when spoken with honesty.

"I'm sorry."

"I forgive you."

Built into the language we use is the divine plan of God, a plan to repair relationships and rebuild what was broken. When used properly and with integrity, someone who has wronged another person has the option to say "I'm sorry." Then, the offended party has the option to release their guilt with the phrase "I forgive you." When this exchange takes place in purity, it can literally be felt.

Forgiveness is a choice and a matter of will. Our introductory passage for this lesson informs us that it is God's will for us to forgive because He has forgiven us. Some have said, "I just can't forgive that person." In truth, they can but choose not to. Others have said, "I will not forgive that person," and they probably won't because their will has superseded God's will. This is why there is so much power in forgiveness. It is a choice we make to set aside our will for the will of God.

As Jesus hung upon the cross, it was forgiveness that was on His lips. Even after He had done nothing to merit such torture, no crime was committed, and nothing was stolen. As He hung there bleeding and His body tormented by pain, He chose to say, "...*Father, forgive them...*" (Luke 23:34 KJV). That forgiveness was so powerful that the Earth shook, the sun was blotted out, and the veil in the Temple was torn from top to bottom. It set His Spirit free, and it can do the same for you.

While it is true that some people will never say they are sorry, God doesn't ask us to wait until they do. True love is proactive and will relentlessly pursue relationship. When Jesus said, *"Father, forgive them..."* He was talking about you and me as well. He was forgiving past, present, and even future injustices against Him because true love is selfless.

But God demonstrates His own love toward us, in that while we were still sinners, Christ died for us.
Romans 5:8 NKJV

I'm sure you're probably thinking of someone right now who has wronged you, someone for whom you have a thousand reasons why they don't deserve forgiveness. Maybe you have forgiven them, but they just keep destroying your trust. You might even ask, "How many times am I supposed to forgive that person?" Well, you're not the first person to ask that. One of Jesus' followers asked Him the same thing: *"Then Peter came to Jesus and asked, 'Lord, how many times shall I forgive my brother who sins against me? Up to seven times?' Jesus answered, 'I tell you, not just seven times, but seventy-seven times!'"* (Matthew 18:21-22 BSB)

PRACTICAL APPLICATIONS:

Is there someone who has wronged you that you need to forgive, or someone you need to say sorry to?
(Write their name/s below and work on that)

_____
_____
_____
_____
_____

How did it make you feel when you decided to make things right?
(Be as descriptive as possible)

_____
_____
_____
_____
_____

What are some boundaries you could set up to protect yourself in the future?
(You can forgive someone and still set healthy boundaries)

_____
_____
_____
_____
_____

LESSON 4

THE POWER OF REPENTANCE

"REPENT THEREFORE, AND TURN BACK, THAT YOUR SINS MAY BE BLOTTED OUT, THAT TIMES OF REFRESHING MAY COME FROM THE PRESENCE OF THE LORD..."

ACTS 3:19 ESV

In the last lesson, we talked a lot about forgiving others. Did you know there is a Biblical theme for forgiving yourself as well? The same freedom you feel when letting go of someone else's past can be felt just as much (*if not more*) by releasing your own past. This teaching, found throughout the Bible, is called "repentance." Let's define what this word means.

> **Repentance** means a sincere turning away, in both the mind and heart, from self to God. It involves a change of mind that leads to action, an about face, a turning around.

Sometimes it is easier to believe that God forgives us than it is to forgive ourselves. Guilt and shame cloud our thoughts as we lay our heads on our pillows at night, pulling old skeletons out of the closet and allowing them to browbeat us until we finally fall asleep with worry on our minds. We constantly rerun old scenarios and ask ourselves, "What if I had just done this differently?" The problem is not resolved, our hearts are still torn, and we wake up the next day, pushing those bones back in the closet again. This is not what God intended for His children. We can rise above this; we can live an empowered life!

Because this is about finding that balance of relationship religion, God is not looking for a big, flowery speech that outlines all the points for which you are sorry. He is more interested in the position of your heart when you ask for forgiveness. If you've lived long enough, you will encounter at least one individual in your life who says they are sorry with their lips, but whose heart and actions do not reflect that sincerity. It's all about honesty.

This is perhaps the best time to discuss what prayer really is and how to pray effectively. Prayer, in its simplest form, is merely communicating with God. That communication can look and sound a lot like a normal conversation you might have with a friend. It requires humility, honesty, and a willingness to listen as well. Just like any good conversation, prayer is not a one-sided interaction.

Try this exercise: pray a little, listen a little, and take your time with it; really linger in the moment. Remember also that we don't have to pray in a certain place or position; He is looking at the posture of your heart.

The disciples of Jesus asked Him to teach them how to pray, and He gave them a great outline in the book of Matthew.

"Our Father in heaven, hallowed be your name. Your kingdom come, your will be done, on earth as it is in heaven. Give us this day our daily bread, and forgive us our debts, as we also have forgiven our debtors. And lead us not into temptation, but deliver us from evil." (Matthew 6:9-13 ESV)

This example was not intended to be recited word for word; rather, it was meant to lay the groundwork and provide an outline for prayer. We should start by giving glory and honor to God, praying that in all things His will is accomplished in our prayers. Next, we thank Him for all He has given us and ask Him to forgive us our wrongdoings. From our last lesson, remember that the forgiveness of our own debts is contingent upon our forgiveness of the debts of others first. Finally, we conclude by asking Him to lead us in His ways, and away from evil.

A champion of prayer and repentance in the Bible is David. Before he ever slew Goliath, he had to win the battle over his sinful heart. He prayed a prayer that I have adopted into my own prayers as well, he prayed about secret sins, and sins that he commits even when he knows they're wrong.

"Who can understand his errors? Cleanse thou me from **secret faults**. Keep back thy servant also from **presumptuous sins**; Let them not have dominion over me..." (Psalm 19:12-13 KJV)

This mindset of being repentant, being humble and forgiving, and his willingness to accept God's instructions and even correction is why God could call him "a man after God's own heart." He messed up, but when he did... he told God he was sorry (*repented*) and worked hard at not doing it again. He was not a quitter either, if he messed up, he kept going. He not only asked God to forgive him, he forgave himself as well. Perhaps that is why his son would pen these words...

> **FOR A RIGHTEOUS MAN FALLS SEVEN TIMES, AND RISES AGAIN, BUT THE WICKED STUMBLE IN TIME OF DISASTER AND COLLAPSE.**
>
> PROVERBS 24:16 AMP

PRACTICAL APPLICATIONS:

What are some things you feel like you need to repent of today?
(Admittance of a problem is the first step to fixing it)

_____
_____
_____
_____
_____

How are you going to include prayer in your life?
(Ease into this and slowly add more time)

_____
_____
_____
_____
_____

What are some prayers that you need God to answer?
(Right them down and then come back to this)

_____
_____
_____
_____
_____
_____

LESSON 5

THE POWER OF BAPTISM

"FOR IN CHRIST JESUS YOU ARE ALL SONS OF GOD, THROUGH FAITH. FOR AS MANY OF YOU AS WERE BAPTIZED INTO CHRIST HAVE PUT ON CHRIST."

GALATIANS 3:26-27 ESV

One of the hardest lessons for some to learn is that life becomes far more rewarding when you simply choose to be yourself. However, many spend their days living in the shadow of what others think, allowing their actions to be dictated by a desire to make someone else happy or to gain another's acceptance. The truth is, God does not make mistakes. He created you the way you are for a reason, and His opinion is the one that matters most.

I have seen people "put on masks" around certain individuals, acting one way in front of one person and another way when with someone else. In fact, I've even heard such individuals referred to as "chameleons." If we're being honest, we all do this to some extent. However, I'm not talking about being on your best behavior when Grandma is around or trying to act more mature in front of someone you admire. Rather, I'm referring to the habit of pretending to be something or someone you're not, simply to give the impression that this façade is the real you.

God sees us as we truly are, no matter what mask we wear. He knows us better than we know ourselves. As we draw closer to Christ, reading His Word, praying, and seeking His guidance in every area of life, we will gradually find the courage to remove these "masks." Over time, we become more at ease with the person He created us to be.

The truth is that we will never be perfect. However, we can strive to become better versions of ourselves. While we can model our lives after many admirable people and perhaps find better footing in doing so, our ultimate model should be the only One who was truly perfect in all His ways. When we pattern our lives after Him, we begin from a much stronger foundation.

If you were to take a document and make copies of it multiple times. Eventually, those reproductions lose definition, degrade in quality, and may eventually become unreadable at all. In the same way, when we try and copy ourselves after everyone around us, who we truly are can lack clarity and authenticity. The greatest example to copy is Jesus Christ. He alone set the standard for how to live and treat others.

> ***For we are God's masterpiece.*** *He has created us anew in Christ Jesus, so we can do the good things he planned for us long ago.*
> *Ephesians 2:10 NLT*

Another way to look at it is like this, essentially we can act as reservoirs, constantly filling ourselves with what we are surrounded by, good or bad. It is needful to choose carefully who is pouring into you and set a safe boundary for your recovery. The Bible puts it this way, *"Be not deceived: evil communications corrupt good manners." (1 Corinthians 15:33 KJV)*

So we've just laid a lot of groundwork for this topic on baptism, and with good reason. When we choose to be baptized into Jesus, it is a very serious and even sacred decision. We are emptying ourselves of our old ways and inviting Him to refill our reservoir with new desires. The old desires, the old conversations, the old ways of living, are to be buried with Him in baptism.

This is why baptism is so powerful. Baptism gives us a clean slate on life. It removes any and all sinful stains from our past, covers us through the redemptive blood of Jesus Christ, and grants us the honor of applying His name to our life. God's ultimate plan and divine purpose for humanity unfolds in our lives personally when we see our need for forgiveness, ask God for that forgiveness, and then put action into our desire to be forgiven by being baptized in His name.

Jesus placed so much emphasis on this topic that He told us in Mark 16 that we cannot be saved without being baptized! He says in Mark 16:16 *"Whoever believes and is baptized will be saved, but whoever does not believe will be condemned."* (KJV) Later, Peter would even liken the waters of baptism to the flood waters of Noah's day that saved Noah and his family from the sinful world that surrounded them.

"...God waited patiently while Noah was building his boat. Only eight people were saved from drowning in that terrible flood. And ***that water is a picture of baptism, which now saves you****, not by removing dirt from your body, but as a response to God from a clean conscience. It is effective because of the resurrection of Jesus Christ."* (1st Peter 3:20-21 NLT)

Have you ever had something that was just weighing on you heavily? Something you said or done that you wish you could take back? You've heard it said before, "once it's done it's done". Well, that's the power of baptism, all that has been said or done, every act that has robbed you of sleep can be washed away and you can lay your head on your pillow at night knowing that your conscience is clear before God. Men may not forgive you, but God can and will!

PRACTICAL APPLICATIONS:

Have you been baptized in Jesus' name?
(How did you feel afterward?)

_____
_____
_____
_____
_____

What are some traits you've acquired from others that don't align with your true self?
(Include a friend in this exercise if need be)

_____
_____
_____
_____
_____

What are some changes you've noticed in your life since you've started striving to follow after Christ?
(Name at least three)

_____
_____
_____
_____
_____

LESSON 6

THE POWER OF THE HOLY SPIRIT

> "BUT YOU WILL RECEIVE POWER WHEN THE HOLY SPIRIT HAS COME UPON YOU, AND YOU WILL BE MY WITNESSES IN JERUSALEM AND IN ALL JUDEA AND SAMARIA, AND TO THE END OF THE EARTH."
>
> ACTS 1:8 ESV

The Holy Spirit, or the Holy Ghost, is the missing link between someone who is living an empowered life and someone who is struggling to gain their footing from day to day. Though the Bible is filled with many essential teachings to overcome every obstacle we encounter, there is no theme more central to the mission of Christ than the interwoven spiritual narratives of the Day of Pentecost.

There are many powerful themes in the Law and the Prophets, the Tabernacle in the wilderness, the Passover, and even the many traditions that laid the groundwork for what was to come, *the Cross*. That long road that led Christ to Calvary was the fuel, and the Cross the catalyst, for what would become the ultimate work of Christ. The reuniting, or atonement, of man to God, and the igniting of holy fire in the hearts of His believers.

In the Old testament, we see a people, in a desperate attempt to remedy their sin, striving to carry God with them on the shoulders of men in the deserts. Families that were giving sacrificially of their best lamb to present a sacrifice to God with the hope that the fire would fall once again and turn their sins back, but only for another year. We see weary priests who toiled day and night to ensure that everything was done to the letter of the law, constantly reminding the people of the conditions of the covenant made with their fathers.

THEN WE SEE *JESUS*.

He begins to preach of a day when the Spirit of God would dwell in temples man did not build. He proclaims that He is the spotless Lamb of God offered once and for all, so that we could be set free from sin through the power of the Holy Ghost. He came not to destroy the law but to fulfill it, and in doing so He would create a New Covenant with mankind that would crush sin once and for all. He came to give us power to overcome, so that we might have life, and have it more abundantly.

> *Yes, to this day whenever Moses is read a veil lies over their hearts. But when one turns to the Lord, the veil is removed. Now the Lord is the Spirit, and where the Spirit of the Lord is, there is freedom.*
> 2nd Corinthians 3:15-17 (ESV)

There was so much power released from the cross when Jesus breathed His last breath that the sun was darkened, the earth shook, and the veil in the temple was torn from top to bottom.

All this would signify to His followers that the power of God, the Holy Ghost, was now accessible to anyone. No longer was your social status, your lineage, or even your sin a barrier of entry to the presence of God. Mercy was no longer hidden from mankind, grace was the rule of law, and in His faithfulness, salvation was open to whosoever will!

The culmination of the finished work of the Cross was the outpouring of a promise that went all the way back to the first Adam and was now reconciled in the last Adam.

This promised power was prophesied in the Old Testament, preached about by Peter on The Day of Pentecost in the New Testament, proclaimed by the Apostles following Pentecost, and that same pattern of Pentecostal power persists even now.

> **IF WE LOOK AT WHAT LED UP TO THE BIRTH OF THE CHURCH AND THE PATTERN THE EARLY CHURCH FOLLOWED. WHY WOULD WE CHANGE ANYTHING?**

Some have minimized the power of the Holy Spirit, saying that it only helps you become a more effective witness. However, it was the power of the Holy Spirit that also healed the lame, opened blind eyes, set captives free who were bound by demonic spirits, and broke the chains of addiction for so many. The fact is, that there is a notable difference in those who allow the work of the Spirit to operate in their lives.

What if I told you that the same supernatural occurrence that happened on The Day of Pentecost, is still happening today? What if I told you that you can have more than just a confession of faith in your relationship with God? It's true! You can have an experience with God that will forever change your life! If you're looking for rest, redemption, restoration, recovery, or all of the above, you can have it in the Holy Spirit.

The same power that was promised by Jesus was not for the perfect. It was not for those that knew the Bible inside and out. It was not exclusive to His chosen people in the land of Israel. It was for you, for your children, and for all that are far away, even as many as the Lord our God will call.

Can you hear it? Can you feel it? Do you see that God is calling for you? If so, you have a promise. Power to overcome!

PRACTICAL APPLICATIONS:

Would you like to be filled with the Holy Spirit? Why?

_____
_____
_____
_____
_____
_____
_____

Have you ever felt the presence of God?
(Write down when and where)

_____
_____
_____
_____
_____
_____

Have you ever witnessed a miracle?
(Write about it below)

_____
_____
_____
_____
_____
_____
_____

LESSON 7

EMPOWERED LIVING

"FOR GOD HATH NOT GIVEN US THE SPIRIT OF FEAR; BUT OF POWER, AND OF LOVE, AND OF A SOUND MIND."

2 TIMOTHY 1:7 KJV

If you have received the Spirit of God, then you have nothing to fear when it comes to your new lifestyle. I'm sure you've heard before, "God's got this!" Although this is true, we must first let go. In fact, if you have not yet received the Holy Spirit, it could be that you're still holding onto something. Many who have come to Christ have clung dearly to things they thought they needed.

For some, it was money; for others, it was their drug of choice, and still others were reluctant to let go of past trauma through the power of forgiveness. However, for many of us, it felt as if that was the one area of our lives where we were in control. For instance, we couldn't always control what happened to us that caused pain, but we could control what we did to numb the pain. This mindset is what traps many people in vicious cycles of drug use. It makes drug use almost feel empowering.

In reality, we build prisons for ourselves everytime we run back to our old ways. Truth is, it's scary to let go of those things that have made us who we are up to this point. Addiction is a lifestyle, and when we move away from that culture, it can seem really scary to leave behind a part of ourselves. At times, some even become addicted to the lifestyle more than their drug of choice. Yet, even in that last statement, we see a powerful truth: as a person in active recovery, we have power over our choices. The fact that you have made it this far is a huge win, and you should be proud of yourself.

This is not something you will hear at many meetings, but drug abuse and alcoholism are more of a spiritual sickness than a physical one. In nearly every case of addiction, the victim of that lifestyle has admitted that they felt as if they were "trying to fill a void." That emptiness people long to fill is not always a direct result of their surroundings, but is often a reflection of the emptiness felt inside. This "God-shaped void," as many have called it, is very real.

Every lesson leading up to this one has been very intentional. We have talked about the main habits and hang-ups that keep that void empty or fill it with unfulfilling substitutions. That said, in this last lesson, we will both reemphasize what leads us to empowered living, and what empowered living truly means for your recovery.

As we've touched on before, we were created in the image of God. When God formed man from the dust of the Earth, He breathed the breath of life into him. It was at that time man became a living soul. That soul's relationship with God was severed in the Garden of Eden when man sinned against God. Since that time, the soul of man has been longing to be reunited with the Creator. However, the penalty and price for sin were far too great for mankind to pay. So God robed Himself in flesh to become the Redeemer of our souls; He paid the ultimate price for our debt of sin, His life for ours.

This forgiveness of our debt (sin) is free for the one who desires freedom. All we have to do is simply enter into a covenant (or relationship) with God. The terms of this agreement are simple. First, you must realize that you have done wrong things that have separated you from God. Then you simply need to tell Him you're sorry and that you want to change. This doesn't have to be ritualistic or formal; it just needs to come from your heart.

At this point, if you have not been baptized, you need to take that next step and follow the example of Jesus and His disciples. Remember, baptism gives you a brand-new, fresh start, a clean slate. Once you come out of the water, or maybe even before you get in, expect that God will fill you with His Spirit. Remember that void? This is God's way of filling it! You will absolutely know that He has because you will begin to speak in a language you don't know!

Now, if you've already experienced that for yourself, then let me tell you that you are in for the experience of a lifetime. Your mindset will change; you will begin to develop new desires, and your life will be forever changed for the better. As you begin this journey, you will also immediately notice that in the midst of all this joy, your adversary is still very present. In fact, in the next few weeks, Satan and his minions are going to throw everything they can at you to try and get you to fall back into your old ways. Be encouraged, though; the Holy Spirit will give you power over these things! Yes, you still have to battle your flesh, but now you're not battling alone.

I promise you, it will get easier. *"...Resist the devil, and he will flee from you."* (James 4:7 KJV) Remember as well that you have a new family that is praying for you, rooting for you, and we are always willing to talk if you need us. This is all a part of walking into the plan and purpose God has for your life.

Consider this: If you ever doubt the effectiveness of the prayers of your peers, Jesus prayed for you as well! You've got this. God's got this. We've got this together. *"And I give myself as a holy sacrifice for them so they can be made holy by your truth. I am praying not only for these disciples but also for all who will ever believe in me through their message."* (John 17:19–20 NLT)

PRACTICAL APPLICATIONS:

What was the most useful part of this class?

_____
_____
_____
_____
_____
_____
_____

Who is your accountability partner?
What have you learned together?

_____
_____
_____
_____
_____
_____

What do your next steps look like to you?
How can we help you achieve that goal?

_____
_____
_____
_____
_____
_____

www.ingramcontent.com/pod-product-compliance
Lightning Source LLC
Chambersburg PA
CBHW061311040426
42444CB00010B/2588